Racial and Ethnic Equality

Sean Connolly

FRANKLIN WATTS
LONDON·SYDNEY

An Appleseed Editions book

First published in 2005 by Franklin Watts

Paperback edition 2007

Franklin Watts
338 Euston Road, London NW1 3BH

Franklin Watts Australia
Level 17/207 Kent Street, Sydney, NSW 2000

© 2005 Appleseed Editions

Appleseed Editions Ltd
Well House, Friars Hill, Guestling, East Sussex TN35 4ET

Designed by Helen James

ISBN 978 0 7496 7647 6

Dewey Classification: 323.11

A CIP catalogue for this book is available from the British Library

Photographs by Corbis (Suzi Altman, Bettmann, CHIN ALLAN/CORBIS SYGMA,
Louise Gubb/CORBIS SABA, Hulton–Deutsch Collection, Brooks Kraft, Bob Krist,
Matthew McKee; Eye Ubiquitous, Reuters, Chuck Savage, Frank Trapper, David Turnley,
Eric Vernazobres), Getty Images (Leonard McCombe/Time & Life Pictures)

Printed in China

Franklin Watts is a division of Hachette Children's Books

Contents

A Shameful History

People often accept cruel behaviour as simply a part of life, as if nothing could be done to prevent it. They might think it is normal when school children mock others who look different or behave in a different way from most of their classmates. Many people assume that, in time, even those children doing the teasing will grow out of this sort of behaviour and look back at it with regret and shame.

But that is not always the case and, throughout history, adults and even whole societies have been cruel to people who were different. Even today, people with mental or physical disabilities face **discrimination** at school, in the workplace or in the world at large. Other groups of people, with a different colour of skin or from a different **ethnic** background, have had similar experiences. Many of the things that we take for granted – the right for people to sit where they like on a bus, the chance to use a public water fountain, the opportunity to go to the local public school – have been denied to people over the years because of the way they looked.

Athenians saw no contradiction in owning slaves while developing the world's first democracy.

The Troubled Past

Throughout history, nations have attacked and conquered other nations, often treating the defeated people as slaves. More than 2,500 years ago, ancient Athens developed the ideas that still define

The real differences among people are in their outlook and ideas – not their physical appearance.

democracy, yet half of the city's population was made up of slaves. Although these slaves had many important jobs – such as teachers and musical instructors – and were usually treated well, they could not vote or own property.

Over time, other societies also limited certain people's freedom, often because they were of a different religion. The word **ghetto** developed in medieval Italy to describe the special section of a city where Jewish people were forced to live. The Mughal Empire in India unravelled in the late 17th century because its Muslim rulers abandoned the practice of religious tolerance. Catholics and Protestants in Europe suffered at each other's hands at about the same time.

What is Race?

What is the difference between an Australian Aborigine, a Norwegian and an Alaskan Inuit? In scientific terms, the answer is simple: nothing. From the number of bones to the most basic building blocks of the human body, genes, human beings are alike. But, unfortunately, humans are not always scientific in their thinking.

For centuries, people believed – and many people still believe – that human beings are divided into clear-cut races, with distinct biological differences to identify each race. This belief is based on **superficial** differences between groups of people from different parts of the world – differences such as skin and hair colour and average height and weight. These differences, added to other ethnic differences such as language, religious beliefs and culture, have convinced many that some groups of people are superior to others.

A Special Case

Despite all of these limits to human rights, those in power still considered the other groups to be fellow humans, worthy of respect. Events from the 15th century onwards, however, introduced a new type of behaviour – an international system of slavery based on race. European countries began to develop **colonies** in North and South America. They needed many people to work on the large farms they established – especially the vast sugar and tobacco **plantations** in warmer parts of the Americas. They forcibly transported millions of African people to America, robbing them of their freedom and way of life. Once in the 'New World', where European immigrants were free to make their fortunes, these African people were bought and sold in the same way that farmers bought and sold tools or crops.

Africans faced disease and terrible discomfort during their long voyage to begin life as American slaves.

Benjamin Banneker

Nearly every African-American in the 18th century was a slave. In some places, however, blacks lived freely if they or their ancestors had been freed. One free African-American man, Benjamin Banneker (1731–1806), spent most of his life on the Maryland farm he had inherited from his father. Banneker taught himself many subjects and became an expert in mathematics and astronomy. When he was 22, he made a clock completely out of wood, carving each gear by hand. His fame spread throughout the colonies and, later, throughout the United States. In 1789, President George Washington appointed Banneker to the commission planning the nation's capital. Three years later, Banneker began publishing a scientific **almanac**. He sent a copy of the first almanac to Thomas Jefferson, along with a letter denouncing slavery and arguing against Jefferson's comments that white people were superior to blacks.

Getting Rich From Slavery

During the colonial period, merchants grew rich from the expanding slave trade. Between 1680 and 1686, two million African slaves passed through British ports on their way to America. Records from 1757 show that the slave trade earned British ports more than £197 million annually in today's prices.

Even colonies with little slavery were able to cash in on this trade. New England had few slaves because its harsh climate and poor soil meant there were few farms to work. But New England merchants prospered from the 'triangular trade.'

They transported slaves from Africa to Britain's sugar-producing colonies in the West Indies. There, the merchants bought sugar and molasses, to be converted into rum back in New England. They then used the rum to buy more slaves.

'Our trade with Africa is very profitable to the nation in general. . . . plantations are the greatest cause of the riches of the kingdom.'

Joshua Gee, British Merchant, 1729.

African families were often split up at American slave auctions.

A 'Peculiar Institution'

The late 18th century saw revolutions in America and France create governments grounded on principles of equality. Writers such as Jean-Jacques Rousseau of France and Edmund Burke of Britain championed the cause of human rights. But at the same time, millions of Africans continued to be sent to America as slaves. Slavery's opponents in European countries began the process of ending the slave trade. But the trade – and slavery itself – continued to flourish in the United States.

It took the hard work of anti-slavery activists and the courage of many slaves themselves to banish slavery in the 'land of the free'. In the end, it was only the bloody conflict of the Civil War (1861–65) that outlawed slavery. But the legacy of this 'peculiar institution', as American slavery was known, would carry on for many years after African Americans were granted their **constitutional** rights as Americans. Some local and state governments in the former slave-owning parts of the South continued to put obstacles in the way of former slaves and their descendants. Many black Americans found it difficult – if not impossible – to find jobs and education, or to register to vote

This oil painting shows African-American slaves among those harvesting hay at George Washington's Mount Vernon estate in Virginia.

Caribbean Triumph

Slaves on Caribbean islands ruled by European countries as colonies sometimes had a better chance of overthrowing slavery than slaves in the United States did. In 1791, slaves in the French colony of Haiti rose up under the leadership of Toussaint L'Ouverture, a self-educated former slave. By 1794, they had driven the French and British from Haiti. Ten years later, Haiti was declared the world's first black **republic**.

Toussaint L'Ouverture led Haitian slaves to victory against Napoleon's French army.

Violent Uprisings

Escaped American slaves were hunted down by dogs and, if caught, they were often shot as an example to other slaves. But this danger did not prevent many slaves from trying to overcome their condition in organized uprisings. Virginian slave Nat Turner led one of the most famous of these uprisings in 1831. Turner led about 80 other slaves in a violent, two-day rebellion that led to the deaths of 60 whites. The number of black deaths – including those executed or **lynched** afterwards – was close to 100. Although the uprising was brief and did little to threaten slavery as a whole, it showed the risks African-Americans were prepared to take to battle the peculiar institution.

Nat Turner was arrested and executed after the 1831 slave uprising in Virginia.

'On this subject (freeing of the slave population) I do not wish to think, or speak, or write with **moderation**. No! No! Tell a man whose house is on fire to give a moderate alarm . . . but urge me not to use moderation in a cause like the present. I am in earnest – I will not equivocate – I will not excuse – I will not retreat an inch – AND I WILL BE HEARD.'

William Lloyd Garrison, writing in the first edition of *The Liberator*, January 1, 1831.

Abolitionists

Many people in Europe and America had opposed slavery since the 16th and 17th centuries. But this opposition did not begin to have a real effect until the 1780s, when William Wilberforce (1759–1833) and other British reformers campaigned to end the slave trade. They appealed to people's religious and moral values by publicizing the inhumane conditions faced by Africans on their journeys into slavery. Britain outlawed the slave trade in 1807, with the United States following a year later. But slavery itself remained as strong as ever in the United States. Some opponents of slavery believed that it would simply die out over time. Extreme opponents, however, saw that the US slave population was growing despite the ban on transporting slaves from Africa. These extreme opponents became known as 'abolitionists', because they called for the abolition, or immediate outlawing, of slavery. The movement gained focus when William Lloyd Garrison founded *The Liberator*, an abolitionist newspaper, in Boston in 1831. Garrison founded the American Anti-Slavery Society two years later.

Abolitionists kept the issue of slavery at the forefront of American politics. *Uncle Tom's Cabin* (1852), an antislavery novel by Harriet Beecher Stowe (1811–96), sold more than 500,000 copies in five years in the United States alone. And extreme abolitionists such as John Brown (1800–59), who used violence as a weapon, helped widen the divisions that led to the Civil War.

Former slaves such as Frederick Douglass, Sojourner Truth (1797–1883), and Harriet Tubman (1820–1913) helped the abolitionist cause with their courage and their firsthand accounts of life as slaves. They and other abolitionists operated the Underground Railroad, a network of 'safe houses' leading escaped slaves northwards to a new life in Canada.

Frederick Douglass

One of the most powerful voices raised against slavery was that of Frederick Douglass (1817–95), a former slave who escaped to Massachusetts in 1838. As a respected member of the Massachusetts Anti-Slavery Society, Douglass travelled through free states (states where slavery was not allowed), powerfully describing the injustices of slavery and the hatred that African-Americans felt for it. Beginning in 1847, he acted as the 'station master' and 'conductor' of the Underground Railroad in Rochester, New York, where he also edited the abolitionist newspaper *North Star*. Douglass helped recruit black troops to fight in the Union Army during the Civil War. After the war, he supported the **constitutional amendments** that granted black American men full citizenship and the right to vote.

Frederick Douglass held a number of government positions and was a respected public speaker.

Escaped slaves, including children, arrive at Leon Coffin's farm, one of the busiest 'stations' of the Underground Railroad.

'I went out and hammered off my chains – found some assistance to get off my cuffs, and came on my way, traveling altogether nights by the north star, and lying by in the day. In Ohio, I found the best kind of friends, and soon reached Canada.'

Escaped slave Harry Thomas, describing how he escaped with help from the Underground Railroad.

The Cost of Freedom

The US Civil War ended in 1865, and the slave-owning states of the **Confederacy** were defeated. That same year, the US Congress passed the 13th Amendment to the Constitution, abolishing slavery throughout the country. The 15th Amendment, which took effect in 1870, granted full voting rights to all American men, including blacks. It seemed that the United States was living up to its ideals – that 'all men are created equal' – at last.

In reality, however, things were very different. Despite the changes occurring nationally, African-Americans and other ethnic groups still faced discrimination at state and local levels. Particularly in the South, blacks were denied the vote through a number of local laws. 'Grandfather clauses' in some state constitutions gave voting rights only to those people whose grandfathers had enjoyed that right in the past – and of course the grandfathers of most African-Americans at that time had been slaves who were not allowed to vote.

Racial division even extended to separate drinking fountains for whites and blacks in the American South.

Discrimination meant that African-Americans in Pensacola, Florida, had to use the rear entrance of this cinema.

Literacy tests also made it hard for poorly educated black people to qualify to vote.

In addition to facing these legal obstacles, black people had to deal with discrimination on other fronts. They were denied jobs and a decent education, forcing them to live in a way that made it almost impossible to make any real progress. This era saw a system of separate facilities set up for blacks and whites, with whites having access to better schools, housing, and transportation. Worst of all was the violence that was unleashed on blacks. The Ku Klux Klan,

Against the Law

African-Americans continued to face widespread legal obstacles in the decades after slavery was abolished in the United States. Despite the changes to the US Constitution, which extended civil rights on a national level, many states kept old laws – or even made new ones – that limited the freedom of black citizens. Below are excerpts from some of these laws, which refer to African-Americans as 'negroes' or 'coloured' people.

'Marriages between a white person and a negro, or between a white person and a person of negro descent to the fourth generation inclusive, are hereby forever prohibited.' (Florida)

'Separate free schools shall be established for the education of children of African descent; and it shall be unlawful for any coloured child to attend any white school, or any white child to attend a coloured school.' (Mississippi)

'Any person . . . who shall rent any part of any such building to a negro person or a negro family when such building is already in whole or in part in occupancy by a white person or white family shall be guilty of a **misdemeanor**.' (Louisiana)

a terrorist organization founded in 1866, attacked those who tried to put new anti-discrimination laws into practice. Mobs of white people attacked blacks and often lynched them in order to scare other African-Americans, with the goal of keeping them from exercising their new rights.

The Ku Klux Klan also attacked lawyers and other white people who supported or enforced laws granting racial equality.

Signals of Change

Despite the hatred of many prejudiced white Americans and the laws that limited civil rights in many parts of the United States, African-Americans had some reason to be hopeful. Some of the black leaders who had been educated in the decades after the Civil War began to develop an organized struggle for equality. The first step was convincing black Americans that the system could be changed, especially if enough people pressed for reform.

John Hope, a professor at Roger Williams University, addressed fellow African-Americans in Nashville, Tennessee, in 1896. He called on them to reject the system that limited their civil rights and their human dignity: 'Rise, Brothers! Come let us possess this land. Never say "Let well enough alone." . . . Be discontented. Be dissatisfied. . . . Let your dissatisfaction break mountain-high against the walls of prejudice and swamp it to the very foundation.'

Hope's stirring speech paved the way for the civil rights movement of the 20th century. It would take nearly seven decades to turn Hope's 'dissatisfaction' into concrete legal changes. But his words, and those of other civil rights pioneers, would continue to inspire people in the mean time.

Ida B. Wells

One of the most active publicists for the cause of civil rights was newspaper editor Ida B. Wells (1862–1931). Wells attended college and accepted a teaching post in Memphis, Tennessee, in the late 1870s. There, she became the co-owner and editor of a black newspaper, *The Free Speech and Headlight*. Wells was a fierce opponent of the discrimination and violence that black Americans faced. She wrote many editorials calling for improved conditions for African-Americans, including better education and voting rights. Wells had stood up for her own rights in a dispute with a railway company, and her editorials called on other black people to be more active. In particular, Wells attacked lynching, which kept many black people from playing a more active role in the civil rights struggle. In 1896, Wells helped organize the National Association of Colored Women, and she later helped found the National Association for the Advancement of Colored People (see pages 17).

For more than five decades, Ida B. Wells played a prominent role in the struggle for racial equality.

The Hard Work Begins

Two prominent African-American men came to represent opposing views of how to achieve equality in the 20th century. The first was Booker T. Washington (1856–1915), the largely self-taught son of a slave. From 1872 to 1875, he studied at the Hampton Institute, a newly established school for black students. In 1881, he took charge of a new school for black students in Tuskegee, Alabama, concentrating on providing industrial and agricultural training. His skill as a teacher and public speaker made him famous across the country. In 1895, Washington urged blacks to agree to a **compromise**: they should accept their lower position in society, while at the same time concentrating on improving their condition through hard work and self-reliance.

Flanked by a symbolic portrait of Lincoln and a tablecloth labelled 'Equality', Booker T. Washington dines with US President Theodore Roosevelt in October 1901.

Historic Concert

The great African-American soprano Marian Anderson gave an outdoor concert at the Lincoln Memorial in Washington, DC, on Easter Sunday 1939. She had tried to book Constitution Hall (the largest concert hall in Washington) but was told that every date she suggested was already taken. The hall was owned by the Daughters of the American Revolution (DAR), whose ancestors had fought against the British. The DAR prohibited blacks from performing there. Leading musicians cancelled their concerts at the hall in protest, and First Lady Eleanor Roosevelt resigned her membership in the DAR. The Department of the Interior (a branch of the federal government) gave Anderson permission to sing at the Lincoln Memorial, and several leading members of the Roosevelt Administration were among the 75,000 who attended. The triumphant concert became a symbol of how determination and protest could overcome racial discrimination.

Marian Anderson at the Lincoln Memorial.

Opposing Washington was another African-American with experience in education. W. E. B. Du Bois (1868–1963) was a brilliant scholar and the first black person to receive a **doctorate** from Harvard University. Du Bois became a university teacher, studying the history and conditions of black Americans. In 1903, he began publicly disputing Washington's views on compromise. Instead, Du Bois argued that African-Americans needed to press hard for changes that would give them the rights they were being denied.

Taking Things Forward

Du Bois's arguments convinced many people – black and white alike – that accepting things as they stood was getting the civil rights movement nowhere. In 1905, Du Bois organized a meeting to plan a way forward. This led to the formation of the National Association for the Advancement of Colored People (NAACP) four years later. The NAACP was to become a leading voice in the civil rights movement, forcing the issue in a number of areas relating to law enforcement and black people's rights under the US Constitution. It also helped individuals who had lost their livelihood due to discrimination or who were wrongly arrested because of unjust laws.

'I think there was extreme resentment among black veterans when they came back [to the United States from fighting in World War II] because they felt, "I paid my dues over there and I'm not going to take this anymore over here".'

James Hicks, a black officer describing how African-American soldiers viewed discrimination when they returned from the war.

Legacies of War

World War II (1939–45) was a turning point for the civil rights movement around the world. People from all ethnic groups joined to fight for democracy, even if laws and customs at home made some of them 'second-class citizens'. Japanese-Americans, for example, were forced from their homes and sent to live in camps during the war.

Japanese Americans held in internment camps spent years away from their homes.

Many ethnic groups were represented in the battle to overcome Japan and Nazi Germany, but they often felt ignored after victory was achieved. The thousands of Indian troops who bolstered Britain's war efforts returned to a country that was not yet independent. Other Asian ex-soldiers faced difficulties in trying to move to Australia after the war because of racially exclusive immigration laws. African and Hispanic Americans – who sometimes could not live next door to white families in America – showed courage and loyalty to the United States fighting in Europe and the Pacific. All of these groups would need to struggle for equality after the war.

'He probably did as much for Hispanic veterans – Hispanics in general – as [Martin Luther] King and [Cesar] Chavez did, mainly in erasing a lot of the stereotypes about Hispanics.'

National Guard Bureau Chief Army Lt.-Gen. Edward Baca, recalling the civil rights efforts of Dr Hector P. Garcia.

Non-violent Protest

One of the most important weapons for civil rights activists in the 20th century was non-violent protest. This tactic was developed by Indian leader Mohandas Gandhi, who became known as Mahatma ('Great Soul') Gandhi. As a young lawyer in British-ruled South Africa, he saw that the Indian population, like the black population, had fewer

rights than whites. He urged Indian South Africans to ignore many of the unfair laws that discriminated against them, but he stressed that their actions must be peaceful. Their non-violent resistance forced the government to change some laws. Gandhi continued this strategy in his native India, which was also controlled by Great Britain. Gandhi recognized that there was strength in numbers, and he organized a series of protests that eventually led to India's independence in 1947.

Mahatma Gandhi (left) and fellow activist Sarojini Naidu lead thousands of Indians on a peaceful anti-British protest in 1930.

CORE Values

African-American James Farmer admired Gandhi's non-violent protest methods and decided to use them in the United States. In 1942, he founded the Congress of Racial Equality (CORE) to fight against discrimination using non-violent methods such as the sit-in. Protesters would stay seated in restaurants, cafés, theatres and buses where black people were supposedly not allowed. In 1947, CORE decided to put to the test a 1946 Supreme Court ruling that outlawed **segregated** seating on interstate buses. A racially mixed group of nine people traveled by bus through several Southern states. Their publicized 'Journey of **Reconciliation**' revealed that discrimination still existed. Several of the black riders were arrested in South Carolina and forced to serve on a **chain gang**.

Public Progress

The United States emerged from World War II as the most powerful country in the world, its booming economy – unlike those of Britain and other European countries – hardly affected by the war. But the issue of racial equality and civil rights was becoming ever more important there. Civil rights activists were impatient for change and saw that the wider public should become more aware of their struggle. The publicity generated by the US civil rights movement attracted the attention of people around the world. And the issues at stake had relevance for Great Britain, with its growing Afro-Caribbean and Asian population, and in Australia, with its own Aboriginal population and thousands of new immigrants arriving each year. Civil rights supporters across the globe took heart in the 1950s, as the United States tackled the problems of segregation in American society. A breakthrough came in 1954, when the Supreme Court ruled that segregation in public schools was **unconstitutional**.

Segregation had once been common on Southern buses, but by 1956, Dr. Martin Luther King, Jr. (second row, left), was able to sit next to Reverend Glenn Smiley, a fellow activist.

The Bus Boycott

The CORE Journey of Reconciliation in 1947 (see page 19) focused on US interstate buses, but local buses in much of the South were still segregated. Black passengers had to sit at the back of a bus, and those in the middle had to give up their seats if the white section filled up. One of the most important incidents in the civil rights movement arose because of this system.

On December 1, 1955, Rosa Parks got on to a bus in Montgomery, Alabama, to go home from work. She took a seat next to three other African-Americans in the middle of the bus. Several stops later, the white section filled up, and a white man needed a seat. The driver called out, 'All right, you folks. I want those seats.' The other three black passengers got up, but Rosa Parks remained in her seat. The driver stopped the bus and called the police who came and arrested her.

Local members of the NAACP paid Rosa Parks's **bail** and began to organize a **boycott** of Montgomery buses by the city's large black population. Church leaders helped with this peaceful demonstration by forming the Montgomery Improvement Association. They chose a 26-year-old minister named Martin Luther King, Jr., to be their leader. King showed his strength as a speaker and organizer, and he drew international publicity for what many saw as a fundamental test of human rights.

While the boycott continued, lawyers representing Rosa Parks took her case to the highest courts in the United States. Finally, on November 13, 1956, the US Supreme Court ruled that segregation on buses was unconstitutional. Inspired by this victory, civil rights leaders organized bus boycotts in other cities, including Birmingham and Mobile, Alabama, and Tallahassee, Florida. Just as importantly, the Montgomery boycott launched the national career of one of America's greatest civil rights heroes: Martin Luther King, Jr.

'We felt that we were somebody, that we had forced the white man to give what we knew was our own citizenship.'

Jo Ann Robinson, recalling her involvement in the Montgomery bus boycott.

It was one thing to know that you had the right to attend a good local school or college. It was quite another thing to be one of the first to put the law to the test. The 1950s saw just such 'tests' carried out, often in the face of violent resistance but also in the public eye. Television, radio and press reports brought these conflicts into people's homes around the world. And with this publicity came international support for those who had been denied their rights.

Showdown in Little Rock

In the years following World War II, the NAACP (see page 17) concentrated on equal educational rights for all Americans. Many US school systems, especially in the South, had 'separate but equal' schools for black students. In most cases, the black schools had fewer teachers and less equipment than the white schools had. Lawyers representing the NAACP took legal action against a number of these school systems. Eventually, the US Supreme Court had to rule whether or not separate but equal schools were legal. In 1954, it decided that this policy was unconstitutional and should be put to an end across the country.

In practice, however, very little changed in the next few years. Things came to a head in September 1957, when Arkansas Governor Orval Faubus defied a federal order to allow nine black students to attend Central High School in Little Rock. President Dwight Eisenhower responded by sending U.S. troops to Little Rock to enforce the order. Millions of television viewers around the world watched as the nine students were escorted into the high school by armed soldiers. After the soldiers returned to their base, the nine students faced a barrage of taunts and threats of violence that lasted throughout the school year. Only one of them, Ernest Green, was in his last year. He graduated on May 29, 1958, becoming a symbol of the courage of the students as a whole.

Jackie Robinson crossed the 'colour barrier' in 1947, when he became the first African-American to play major league baseball (for the Brooklyn Dodgers). Despite taunts and threats, he soon showed himself to be a skilled player. Robinson won the National League batting title in 1949 and was named the league's Most Valuable Player that same year.

'When they called my name, there was nothing, just the name, and then there was eerie silence. Nobody clapped. But I figured they didn't have to because after I got that diploma, that was it. I had accomplished what I had come there for.'

Ernest Green, describing the graduation ceremony at Little Rock's Central High School on May 29, 1958.

A Message of Hope

While postwar America faced up to the issue of racism, great social changes were taking place elsewhere in the world. As many colonies in the **developing world** struggled for independence (see page 25) and equal rights within their countries, European countries began to see racial unrest within their own borders.

Many immigrants from former colonies in Asia, Africa, the Caribbean and Ireland helped Britain rebuild its economy after the war. France saw waves of people arrive, especially from Algeria and other areas formerly under French control. Germany welcomed many 'guest workers' from other countries, especially Turkey. These newcomers and their children soon faced opposition. Some European workers resented what they saw as competition for their jobs.

This opposition often showed itself in ugly forms of discrimination. People from ethnic minorities became victims of violence and found it hard to get jobs or even housing. A sign, once common in British boarding houses in the 1950s, spelled out this offensive message: 'No Blacks, Irish or Dogs'.

A black man shines shoes in central London in the 1950s. Non-white immigrants to Britain – especially Afro-Caribbeans – found it hard to get better jobs in their new country.

Colonial Struggles

Beginning in the 16th and 17th centuries, a number of European countries set up colonies in other places around the world. The colonies provided the 'mother countries' with important goods for trade, such as food, timber and minerals. And the local populations of these countries could be made to work for less money than people at home, enabling the European countries to become richer.

Many European countries saw establishing colonies as the only way to develop themselves and to compete with their European neighbours. Over the course of two centuries, Spain, Portugal, Great Britain, France, Sweden, the Netherlands, Germany and even Belgium had become colonial powers.

European colonies fell into two main categories. Some, such as most colonies in North and South America, were places where immigrants from the mother country arrived to set up new lives. Others, like most colonies in Africa and Asia, were lands where a small number of Europeans ruled over much larger native populations.

In the 18th and 19th centuries, most colonies in North and South America (including the United States) became independent. Other places, however, remained under the control of European powers well into the 20th century. In many such colonies, the struggle for political independence became a vital element in the fight for racial and ethnic equality. The black or Asian majority in these nations sought to replace the rule of a white minority representing another country.

Margaret Thatcher, then British prime minister, visits a housing development in Hong Kong in 1984, the same year Britain agreed to return the colony to Chinese rule in 1997.

The Fight Against Apartheid

South Africa, like most other African nations, was ruled for many years by European countries. Dutch and, later, British rule finally ended in the middle of the 20th century. But independent South Africa held on to the system known as apartheid, under which the white minority controlled the country and nonwhites had few rights.

Black and Indian South Africans, along with their white allies, tried for decades to overturn this system. The African National Congress (ANC) and other civil rights organizations led demonstrations that were often crushed violently by the South African police and army.

Nelson Mandela and other important ANC leaders were convicted of treason in 1964 and sentenced to life in prison. Mandela delivered a long speech at their trial, in which he outlined his hopes for a democratic, nonracial government that would replace the unjust apartheid system. He retained his beliefs during his long period in prison. Although

Mandela had little or no contact with the outside world, people in South Africa and around the world came to view him as a symbol of freedom and courage.

World opinion had swung firmly against the South African government by the 1980s. The government was forced to remove some of its apartheid laws, and it promised Mandela his freedom if he would accept this move as a compromise. Mandela stood firm. The South African government finally freed Mandela in 1990, promising an end to apartheid and full voting rights for all South Africans. The country's first democratic elections were held in 1994, and Nelson Mandela was elected president. He devoted much of his five-year term to building bridges among all of the ethnic communities – black, white, and Indian – in his country.

More than 20 years after Mandela's arrest, South African police were still violently attacking protesters calling for his release.

A Message of Hope

Nelson Mandela was sworn in as South Africa's first democratically elected president on May 10, 1994. As president, Mandela called for racial harmony in his 'rainbow nation'.

The Freedom Charter

On June 26, 1955, more than 3,000 South Africans from all races adopted a statement of anti-apartheid goals that inspired people not only in their own country, but also around the world. The opening words of the Freedom Charter, aimed squarely at the white government of South Africa, are a challenge to anyone who would deny basic civil rights to a nation's entire population:

'We, the People of South Africa, declare for all our country and the world to know: that South Africa belongs to all who live in it, black and white, and that no government can justly claim authority unless it is based on the will of all the people; that our people have been robbed of their birthright to land, liberty and peace by a form of government founded on injustice and inequality; that our country will never be prosperous or free until all our people live in brotherhood, enjoying equal rights and opportunities; that only a democratic state, based on the will of all the people, can secure to all their birthright without distinction of colour, race, sex or belief.'

'We Shall Overcome'

The 1960s were a time of great social change throughout the world. People who were born in the 'baby boom' just after World War II were now old enough to judge the world around them and – more importantly – work to improve it. African-Americans, European minorities, and newly independent countries all felt this new spirit of the times. In the United States, where so much of the civil rights struggle was concentrated, thousands of volunteers joined in the effort to overthrow the obstacles faced by minorities.

Although many groups and individuals took part in this campaign, most Americans saw one man – Dr Martin Luther King, Jr. – as the leader of the movement. King had already proved himself to be a tireless supporter of fellow African-Americans in the 1950s. In those days, he led dozens of people in stubborn demonstrations, boycotts and prolonged court battles. By the 1960s, he was leading thousands of people in peaceful marches through some of the

Protest marches included calls to support the Mississippi Freedom Democratic Party (MFDP), which had been formed to challenge the exclusion of blacks from the state's regular Democratic Party.

'Freedom Summer'

Many civil rights activists in the early 1960s believed that voting changes would be the best way to push their movement ahead. African-Americans needed to be able to vote for public officials who would work for change – and to vote against those who resisted it. There was a real problem, though. In some parts of the South, fewer than 40 per cent of black adults were registered to vote. Standing in their way were laws and limits that made it almost impossible for African-Americans to register in some places.

In 1961, 26-year-old African-American teacher Robert Moses led a group of volunteers from the Student Nonviolent Coordinating Committee (SNCC) to the South in order to teach blacks there how to overcome the obstacles that kept them from registering to vote. The registration drive made slow progress for several years until Moses recruited 900 additional volunteers in 1964. This new effort, called the 'Freedom Summer', soon made headlines – for tragic reasons. Three volunteers, one black and two white, were killed in Mississippi as part of a white backlash. The tragedy, however, did have some positive effects. International attention focused on the voter-registration drive, encouraging more volunteers to join the drive and increasing the success rate of the campaign. In the end, thousands of African-Americans registered to vote for the first time. As civil rights activist James Bevel put it, 'black people were fighting for more than a seat at the lunch counter; they were fighting for seats in the **legislature**.'

most segregated parts of the American South. His triumphant and inspirational rally in Washington, DC, in 1963 (see page 30) showed the confidence and optimism of black Americans and their supporters.

The African-American spiritual 'We Shall Overcome', sung on most of these marches, summed up the longing and hope of those who marched,

'I Have a Dream'

In August 1963, more than 200,000 civil rights supporters marched peacefuly across the Mall to the Lincoln Memorial in Washington, DC. The year 1963 was significant, since it was exactly 100 years after President Lincoln's Emancipation Proclamation, which had granted freedom to African-American slaves living in the rebelling Confederate states.

The keynote, or opening, speaker was Dr Martin Luther King, Jr. Dr King's speech electrified the crowd, as he repeated the phrase 'I have a dream' to introduce rousing messages of hope and equality. In his speech, Dr King said, 'I have a dream that my four little children will one day live in a nation where they will be judged not by the colour of their skin, but by the content of their character.'

demonstrated, and campaigned for change. It symbolized the struggle itself, even when there were setbacks. By 1965, Dr King and others like him had succeeded in lifting the last bars that blacks faced in voting. He then led the movement to another problem area: poverty across the nation. Dr King was involved in this campaign when an assassin's bullet killed him in 1968. Despite the tragic loss of its devoted leader, the movement was able to continue and build on the successes that King and other activists had achieved.

Martin Luther King, Jr., won the Nobel Peace prize in 1964 for leading the black struggle for equality through non-violence.

'Is this America, the land of the free and the home of the brave where we have to sleep with our telephones off the hooks because our lives are threatened daily because we want to live as decent human beings in America?'

Fannie Lou Harper, civil rights voting activist, speaking in 1964.

Turning Progress into Law

In the mid-1960s, President Lyndon Johnson and the US Congress began the process of turning the progress of the civil rights movement into law. The Civil Rights Act of 1964 made segregation in public facilities and discrimination in employment illegal. The Voting Rights Act of 1965 responded to the problems that had triggered the Freedom Summer voting drives. This law suspended the use of literacy tests and other obstacles facing potential black voters. Within several years, African-Americans were helping to shape the face of Southern politics, and by the early 1970s, they began to be elected as representatives to the US Congress in districts where blacks were in the majority.

The Jewish Contribution

Jewish people can look back to their own long history for countless examples of discrimination and hatred. Throughout the world, the Jewish community has had to deal with widespread **anti-Semitism**. This experience has enabled many Jews to understand the position of other groups facing similar discrimination. Jews were at the forefront of the US civil rights movement in the 1960s, joining Freedom Rides and civil rights demonstrations and risking their lives to show their support for African-Americans. Two such Jewish supporters of African-American rights were Andrew Goodman and Michael Schwerner. These two young men were assisting African-American James Chaney in investigating the bombing of a church in rural Mississippi when they – along with Chaney – were murdered by racists. Their deaths showed that racism was a deadly force aimed not just at blacks but at all Americans who supported the black cause.

The parents of murdered civil rights activist Michael Schwerner join African-American leaders at a political demonstration just weeks after their son's body was found in August 1964.

Other Groups, Other Causes

Martin Luther King's message of non-violent protest, itself inspired by Mahatma Gandhi, spread beyond the African-American civil rights movement. In South Africa, where Gandhi had once practised law, people of all races took part in demonstrations in support of the Freedom Charter (see pages 26–27) and the cause of racial equality. Trevor Huddleston, an Anglican priest from Britain, was one of many prominent supporters of the peaceful struggle against apartheid. Within the United Kingdom itself, the civil rights issue became prominent in Northern Ireland, where the Catholic minority (sometimes called 'Nationalists') began to organize themselves to overthrow laws that discriminated against them. Many nationalists sang the American civil rights anthem 'We Shall Overcome' in marches that attracted supporters from all over Britain.

American civic leaders, mobilizing support for Asians, Hispanics and other groups, saw that non-violence could achieve progress. One such leader was Cesar Chavez (1927–93), whose tenacious labour-rights struggle inspired America's Hispanic community. Chavez formed a **trade union** for migrant farm workers, and in 1965 his union supported a **strike** called by Filipino grape pickers in California. In 1968, Chavez went on a publicized 25-day fast and then called for a worldwide boycott of Californian grapes. His non-violent strategy eventually achieved results, and he emerged as a powerful civil rights leader.

Cesar Chavez took the lead in a number of high-profile campaigns, such as this boycott of Safeway supermarkets in 1973.

Voices of Anger

It is not surprising that a long struggle to achieve basic human rights would lead to heated disputes within the cause. Some African-Americans felt that the pace of change was too slow. The non-violent approach of Dr Martin Luther King, Jr., and his supporters had certainly achieved some concrete results. But other black voices, notably that of Malcolm X in the United States, felt that more needed to be done to make change happen.

Others took to the streets in uncontrolled – and often violent – protests about poor living conditions in the heart of many American cities. Thirty-four people died in riots that erupted in Watts, a poor district of Los Angeles, in 1965. Two years later, there were riots in several other US cities, including Newark, New Jersey, where 26 people died. American cities saw even more rioting in the spring of 1968 after the murder of Martin Luther King, Jr.

'Whoever heard of a **revolution** where they lock arms . . . singing 'We Shall Overcome'? Just tell me. You don't do that in a revolution. You don't do any singing; you're too busy swinging. It's based on land. A revolutionary wants land so he can set up his own nation, an independent nation.'

Malcolm X, speaking in Detroit, Michigan, on November 10, 1963.

An armed police officer protects firefighters battling blazes that began during riots in Detroit, Michigan, in July 1967.

Malcolm X

With his forceful personality and fiery speeches, Malcolm X (1925–65) represented a far more aggressive approach to the civil rights struggle than the one adopted by Martin Luther King, Jr. Malcolm X was born Malcolm Little, the son of a Baptist minister in Nebraska. His father was murdered in 1931 after receiving threats from the Ku Klux Klan. His mother then suffered a nervous breakdown. Like his seven brothers and sisters, Malcolm lived for a while in foster homes. He moved to Massachusetts in the eighth grade and was soon drawn into a life of petty crime. In 1946, Malcolm was convicted of burglary and sent to prison. There he came across the works of Elijah Muhammad, the leader of the Black Muslims, also called the Nation of Islam. The Black Muslims called for a radical separation of the races in America as the only way blacks could advance. By the time he was released from prison in 1952, Malcolm had joined the Black Muslims and had taken the name Malcolm X.

By the early 1960s, Malcolm X had become the leading spokesman of the Black Muslims. In speech after speech, he called for achieving equality 'by any means necessary', an attitude that raised the threat of violence. In 1964, Malcolm X left the Black Muslims and founded a non-religious black group, the Organization of Afro-American Unity. Later that year, he made the hajj (Muslim holy pilgrimage) to Mecca, Saudi Arabia. That trip caused him to reconsider some of his views, and he returned to the United States with a message of peaceful unity for African-Americans. However, he had little time to spread this message; the next year, he was shot and killed while making a speech in New York City.

The Black Panthers

Some African-Americans in the mid-1960s believed that the government would never change its mind on basic issues and that the only way to achieve full freedom was through violent revolution. In 1966, Huey P. Newton and Bobby Seale founded the Black Panthers. Set up as a militant political party, the Black Panthers called on all African-Americans to arm themselves to take part in the violent struggle for freedom. By the late 1960s, several party members were involved in violent confrontations with the police, resulting in deaths on both sides. Widely publicized trials resulted, dragging on for years as courts failed to reach a verdict. During this time, the Black Panthers came under intense pressure from other black leaders to abandon violence. In 1972, Newton and Seale pledged to do so; both left the party two years later. Without these strong personalities to lead them, the Black Panthers lost influence and faded from the scene.

Silent Protest

One of the most famous images from the 1968 Olympic Games, held in Mexico City, showed two American athletes raising black-gloved fists in a Black Power salute. Tommie Smith and John Carlos had won the gold and bronze medals in the 200-metre dash. During the medal ceremony, while the 'Star Spangled Banner' played, each man bowed his head and raised his gloved fist as a silent protest against discrimination in the US. Smith later said that his right, gloved fist represented black power in America, while Carlos's left fist represented unity in black America. Smith's black scarf represented black pride, and their black socks (and no shoes) represented black poverty in America. The men were disciplined by the US Olympic Committee and sent home, but not before millions of television viewers around the world saw the divisions facing American society.

'Rivers of Blood'

In the 1960s, the British government responded to the growing problems of discrimination (directed mainly at Asian and black immigrant communities) with a series of Race Relations Acts. These acts made it illegal to deny people basic rights – such as housing, work or education – because of their race or ethnic background. But not everyone in Britain was happy with these changes.

In April 1968, Enoch Powell, a leading member of the governing Conservative Party, made an angry speech against further immigration. In his speech, Powell referred to the words of the ancient Roman poet Virgil, who foresaw Rome's River Tiber running red with blood because of a looming war. Powell's speech – in which he made a similar prediction if nonwhite immigration continued – became known as the 'Rivers of Blood' speech. It upset leaders of Britain's main political parties, causing Powell to lose his position in the government. But it acted as a rallying cry for racist organizations, such as the National Front, to begin calling for repatriation of nonwhite immigrant populations – sending them 'home' to Africa, Asia or the Caribbean.

A black Londoner walks past graffiti supporting Enoch Powell soon after Powell's explosive 'Rivers of Blood' speech.

Continuing Battles

Those who continue the campaign to secure and protect basic human rights find new challenges each year. The world is changing quickly, but the problems of hostility, discrimination, and violence remain – even if the targets have changed. Air travel and other forms of transport have made it easier for people to settle in new countries. Some people have left their own countries freely and have found work and housing in other places. Other people – often called **asylum** seekers – fear for their lives in their homelands. For them, a move is more than a decision to find a better job; it might mean the difference between life and death.

Whether these newcomers are Asian people arriving in France or Britain, or Hispanic workers crossing the US-Mexico border, they have similar stories to tell once they arrive. Many are fearful about being sent home, so they accept the so-called protection of people who offer them jobs illegally. At the start of the new century, it is this movement of people – and the dangers they face both at home and in their new countries – that demands attention.

Soviet Jews arrive in Israel to escape racial hatred in December 1990.

Racism and Politics

The obstacles faced by immigrants to European countries can go far beyond the insults and name-calling of the 1950s. British grocers of Asian descent have found their windows broken and their shops burned. A gang of French youths murdered a young Algerian on a train in 1983; four years later, a Tunisian immigrant was murdered under similar circumstances. Immigrants have also been attacked in Belgium, Italy, Germany, and many other countries. Jewish and Roma (Gypsy) people have been forced from their homes in Central and Eastern Europe.

With these attacks has come the rise of political parties that support racist views. The National Front regularly wins votes in French elections. The British National Party, although smaller, also stirs up anti-immigrant feelings among voters. And parties with ominous similarities to Hitler's **Nazi** Party have sprung up in Austria, Germany and other European nations.

Learning From Hate

The 1995 film *La Haine (The Hate)* is a stark look at hatred and violence in inner-city France. In 2001, the Anglo-Asian band Asian Dub Foundation provided a soundtrack to accompany the film. The meeting of several cultures – French, English, Indian and Jamaican – in the film and its music showed how universal the film's message was. And the unique combination of reggae, dub and drum and bass gave a cutting-edge feel to the age-old message.

French rapper Diam's gives the 'SOS-Racisme sign' during the celebration concert for the organization's 20th anniversary.

Targeting Youth

Many anti-racist organizations have based successful campaigns on educating young people about discrimination and mobilizing them in the fight for equality. Youth Against Racism in Europe (YRE), a London-based organization, helps people in Britain and throughout Europe learn more about the contributions made to society by a wide range of people.

The French anti-racist organization SOS-Racisme began aiming its message at young people in the 1980s. Its slogan, *touche pas à mon pote* ('hands off my friend'), targeted those who would use violence against minorities in France. The French also tapped the power of popular music to get the message across.

As war rocked the region in the 1990s, many Roma people fled Kosovo to escape violence and discrimination.

Terror and Hate

The terrorist attacks on New York City and Washington, DC, on September 11, 2001, shocked the United States and the world at large. But the thousands of innocent victims of those attacks were not the only casualties of the outrage. Within days, some Americans were targeting Arabs – or people they believed to be Arabs – in a series of racially motivated revenge attacks.

Within two days of 9/11, the Council on American-Islamic Relations received more than 300 reports of harassment and abuse. These reports ranged from accounts of families being spat at, to assaults on businesses and individuals. There were even cases of murder. Balbir Singh Sodhi, 49, a petrol station owner from India, was shot dead while landscaping outside his business in Mesa, Arizona. Sodhi was not a Muslim but a Sikh. Many Americans associate Sikhs – because of their turbans and beards – with Muslim terrorist leader Osama bin Laden, who claimed responsibility for the 9/11 attacks.

Tidal Tragedy

On February 5, 2004, tragedy struck the English coastal town of Morecombe when an onrushing tide drowned 20 young men. The men, all Chinese immigrants, had been gathering shellfish – an important local industry worth £5.5 million a year. Some people involved in the industry hire illegal immigrants, threatening to tell the authorities (probably leading to arrest) if the workers complain about their pay. The tragedy has forced British people to re-examine how their society treats newcomers, whether they have arrived legally or not. In that way, it echoes the debate about the position of illegal Hispanic workers in the United States.

Feeling the Heat in Australia

More than 90 per cent of Australia's population is white, tracing its ancestry to Europe. The original settlers of Australia, known as Aborigines, now number about 400,000 – or only 4 percent of Australia's total population. Like other **First Peoples**, the Aborigines faced discrimination before and after their country gained independence. They were forced from many of their lands and found it hard to get good jobs, housing or education.

A series of government measures begun in the 1970s has improved conditions for Aborigines, although many of them now live in **ghettos** in Sydney and other major cities. Many of these city dwellers complain of brutal treatment by police. In February 2004, a 17-year-old Aborigine died in a bicycle accident in Redfern, a Sydney ghetto. Many local people accused the police of chasing the boy and causing his accident. That night, about 100 Aboriginal rioters set fire to the local train station and damaged cars and property in Redfern. Hundreds of police officers in full riot gear doused the rioters with high-pressure hoses, while Aboriginal youths pelted the officers with stones. The street battle ended after nine hours, but tensions between the authorities and the Aboriginal population remained. Some Aboriginal leaders – although they helped calm the disturbance – pointed out that the underlying resentment of their population toward the white-dominated government remains a major issue.

'It's got to stop, the way they treat our kids. They treat our kids like dogs. . . . they manhandle them.'

Gail Hickey, mother of 17-year-old Thomas Hickey, whose death triggered the February 2004 riots in Sydney, Australia.

The Way Forward?

By the end of the 20th century, many countries had taken steps to stamp out the legacy of racial discrimination. These measures need to be examined constantly and strengthened when it becomes clear that a particular group of people is not being treated equally.

But the gains of the civil rights struggle have not been based simply on laws forcing prejudiced people to behave more fairly. The real gains have come from a change in people's attitudes. This basic change was necessary, for example, before the dramatic civil rights legislation of the 1950s and 1960s could even be considered. And people's attitudes still need to be changed.

Visibility is the key to much of this change. Racial prejudice stems from people thinking that other groups are different and out of place in certain situations. Black faces were once thought to be out of place in certain bus seats, public toilets or suburbs. That is no longer the case. Societies must now look ahead to a time

Condoleezza Rice (left) succeeded fellow African-American Colin Powell as US Secretary of State in 2005.

Martin Luther King, Sr., watches as US President Jimmy Carter presents the Medal of Freedom, to his son's widow, Coretta, in July 1977.

Martin Luther King Day

Martin Luther King, Jr., was assassinated in 1968, but his legacy continues to inspire those who want justice and equality around the world. King was awarded the Presidential Medal of Freedom – the highest honour in the United States – **posthumously** in 1977. Nine years later, the US Congress established a federal holiday to honour him. Martin Luther King Day is the third Monday in January.

when a black, brown or yellow face will no longer seem out of place leading the armed forces, a major corporation or even the nation. People of all races benefit from seeing role models from minority groups filling such positions capably.

The gains from the civil rights struggle go far beyond the boundaries of the countries where they have been achieved. If the people of a country have respect for their fellow citizens – regardless of their race or ethnic background – then the country can look at the rest of the world with fresh eyes. Too often in the past, countries have been prepared to go to war with each other because they were 'different'. By seeing beyond the differences, governments can learn to understand other countries. And, with a little understanding, the problems between countries may seem less difficult to resolve peacefully.

The 'Shackled Runner'

In the decades since civil rights legislation was passed in many countries, people from ethnic minorities have been able to excel in many areas that were once blocked to them, including sports, entertainment and other, high-profile, areas. People want to watch the best football player or listen to the finest singer, whatever the colour of their skin. But other areas – notably higher education and the **judicial** system – have been harder for minorities to enter.

Some people believe that every area of society should reflect the makeup of the overall population – that the country would be fairer with more black or Asian judges, teachers, and government officials. They call for **positive discrimination** to help people from minorities break into new fields. British political parties, for example, now actively seek candidates from ethnic minorities.

US President Lyndon Johnson supported **affirmative action** as a way of building on the **Great Society** laws he proposed. He compared competition for jobs to a 100-yard dash between two runners. One of the runners (representing black people's history of slavery) has his legs shackled together. He has completed only 10 yards by the time the other runner (representing white people) has run 50 yards. Then the race is stopped and the shackles are removed (representing the civil rights advances of the 1960s). Some people would argue that things had become equal. But Johnson pointed out that one runner was still 40 yards behind. Affirmative action, in his view, was like helping that runner make up the 40 yards so that the race would be fair when it resumed.

Other people oppose positive discrimination. They feel that it that gives an unfair advantage to people in certain groups, including minorities. They believe everyone should be regarded equally when applying for a job and that whether someone is white or a minority should not have any effect – either positive or negative – on the hiring process.

Oscar Triumphs

The Academy Awards, or 'Oscars', honour the finest motion picture performers. The 2002 award ceremony was an emotional triumph for three African-American actors. On that evening, Halle Berry won the Best Actress award, and Denzel Washington was named Best Actor. They were the first African-Americans to win these top awards since Sidney Poitier in 1963. Poitier also received a special Oscar for his lifetime contribution to the film industry. Backstage, Berry said, 'It's a great night. I never thought it would be possible in my lifetime. I hope this means that they won't see our colour. I think that's what makes us so unique. I think that maybe now we'll start to be judged on our merit and our work.'

'I accept this award in memory of all the African-American actors and actresses who went before me in the difficult years, on whose shoulders I was privileged to stand to see where I might go.'

Sidney Poitier, accepting his Academy Award for Lifetime Achievement in 2002.

Education has been at the core of many social struggles around the world. Seeing successful and respected university lecturers can inspire new generations of ethnic minorities to flourish in all walks of life.

Marino Branch
Brainse Marglann Mhuirí
Tel: 8336297

Glossary and Suggested Reading

affirmative action   another name for positive discrimination (see below)

almanac   a book containing scientific information about a range of subjects

anti-Semitism   discrimination or hostility towards Jewish people

asylum   safety or protection from dangers

bail   money paid by an arrested person to be released from jail until a trial takes place

boycott   the refusal to do business with a person or company as a form of protest

chain gang   jailed people forced to do hard labour, often while chained together

colonies   parts of the world that are governed by a foreign country

compromise   settlement of a dispute in which both sides give in a bit

Confederacy   the 11 southern states that declared their independence from the
   United States in 1861, triggering the Civil War

constitutional   following the principles of a country's constitution

constitutional amendments   official changes to a constitution

democracy   a form of government in which the people, or their elected representatives,
   have power

developing world   countries that rely on basic farming rather than on developed
   industries for their income

discrimination   treating people poorly because of their appearance, ethnicity or gender

doctorate   the most advanced qualification a university provides

ethnic   sharing a common culture or background

First Peoples   a term to describe the people whose ancestors were already living in
   a country when the first Europeans settled there

ghetto   a special (and often poor) part of a city or town where people of a certain
   group are forced to live

Great Society   the name of a programme of civil rights measures proposed by
   US President Lyndon Johnson

Hispanic   coming from a country with a Spanish-speaking culture

internment   keeping people confined because the government is suspicious of them

judicial   the branch of government dealing with courts and the justice system

legislature   the lawmaking branch of government, usually consisting of an assembly of elected
   officials

literacy tests   tests for ability to read and write, often used to deny poorly educated people
   the chance to vote

lynched   put to death illegally, often by hanging

misdemeanour   a minor crime that is usually punished by a fine rather than time in jail

moderation   unwillingness to become too extreme

Nazi   the name of the political party of Adolf Hitler and his followers in Germany during the 1930s and 1940s

plantations   large farms that grow a single crop

positive discrimination   giving certain groups of people an advantage in achieving certain positions because of previous difficulties the groups faced

posthumously   occurring after someone's death

reconciliation   bringing together people, or groups of people, who have been in dispute

republic   a type of government in which representatives are elected to act on behalf of the voters

revolution   the violent overthrow of a country or political system

segregated   kept apart by law

strike   the refusal of a group of workers to continue working until their demands are met

superficial   having to do with the surface and not underlying qualities

trade union   an organized group of workers banding together to improve their working conditions

unconstitutional   going against the principles of a constitution

Further Reading

Erickson, Paul. *Daily Life on a Slave Plantation.* Oxford: Heinemann, 1999.

O'Connor, Maureen. *Equal Rights.* London and Sydney: Franklin Watts, 2000.

One day we had to run (Refugee children tell their stories in words and paintings). London: Evans Brothers in association with UNHCR and Save the Children, 1999.

Tilley, Glennette. *Take A Walk In Their Shoes.* London: Puffin, 1992

Web Sites

Community Relations Commission (UK)

www.cre.gov.uk

The Runnymede Trust (UK)

www.runnymedetrust.org

Anti-Discrimination Commission (Australia)

www.nt.gov.au.adc

Australian Civil Liberties Union

http://go.to/aclu

Index